Original title:
Sunlight and Sprouts

Copyright © 2025 Creative Arts Management OÜ
All rights reserved.

Author: Vivienne Beaumont
ISBN HARDBACK: 978-1-80581-861-8
ISBN PAPERBACK: 978-1-80581-388-0
ISBN EBOOK: 978-1-80581-861-8

Elysian Growth Under the Glare

In a garden wide, a plant did dance,
Wiggling its leaves, taking a chance.
A butterfly tripped over a bloom,
Swaying and laughing in nature's room.

A tree wore spectacles, looking quite wise,
Claiming it missed all the goodbyes.
The flowers giggled, swaying in jest,
While veggies competed for who grew best.

A worm in the dirt, quite a cheeky chap,
Started a clubhouse, grabbing a map.
"Let's host a party!" it shimmied with glee,
As carrots and radishes joined in for tea.

With a wink and a grin, the ants marched in,
Crafting a banquet—oh, let's begin!
In this lively patch, laughter took flight,
Under the gaze of the bright daylight!

Petals in the Embrace of Heat

When the rays tickle blooms,
They giggle in bright hues.
Dancing like silly fools,
In petal-sized cartoon views.

Worms wriggle, laughing loud,
With flowers wearing a proud shroud.
Bees buzz, a choir so sweet,
As they cha-cha to the heat.

Nature's Canvas Aglow

The trees wear their best suits,
In colors like fruity flutes.
Leaves rustle with cheeky grins,
Like gossiping leafy twins.

A painter's palette spills wide,
With colors that spryly glide.
Blades of grass start to jive,
As laughter helps them thrive.

The Breath of New Life

Tiny seeds break out of sleep,
With giggles they start to leap.
Roots tickle underground friends,
A shindig that never ends.

They pop up, all shy and neat,
Making sure they have two left feet.
Roots and shoots sway in delight,
Chasing bugs, while avoiding fright.

Growth in the Gentle Light

Soft beams kiss the tiny green,
Silly sprouts stretch and preen.
They tickle the air all day,
In their own quirky way.

Chasing shadows, playing tag,
Little leaves wave a bright flag.
In this frolicsome parade,
Nature's jokes never do fade.

Awakening Light

The rooster crows a silly tune,
While daisies dance beneath the moon.
Worms in hats twist and snout,
Saying, "We're here! Come check us out!"

Tickled blades of grass do sway,
As giggling flowers greet the day.
A beetle spins, a little round,
Claiming the garden as his town.

Tender Green Beginnings

Tiny leaves peek through the ground,
With whispers of joy, they bounce around.
A ladybug struts all prim and proud,
Claiming her throne, beneath the cloud.

Insects debate who's cooler still,
While ants march by with a marching thrill.
"Oh, what a show!" says one bright sprout,
"Can you believe their silly clout?"

Golden Rays on Young Leaves

Golden hugs from way up high,
Make flowers giggle, oh my, oh my!
A sunflower grins, just like a clown,
While petals twirl in a froggy gown.

"Leafy party!" shouts a pine,
"I swear we'll have the best time of our lives!"
As branches sway, the fruit just grins,
Saying, "Let the leafy laughter begin!"

The Dance of Dawn's Embrace

Dewdrops sparkle like tiny gems,
As sleepy buds bear witness to them.
A frog leaps in a joyous dash,
While crickets play, oh what a clash!

Dandelions twirl, feeling quite bold,
With tales of adventures waiting to unfold.
So let's not sit, it's time to groove,
For all around us, the fun's on the move!

A Harmony of Green in Day's Embrace

In a garden where the daisies dance,
A joke is whispered, giving plants a chance.
The carrots wear capes, thinking they're sly,
While radishes chuckle, oh my, oh my!

The peas are in suits, looking so neat,
They gossip and giggle, what a treat!
The lettuce is laughing at a snail's slow race,
In this lively patch, all keep their place!

Prismatic Growth Beneath the Sky

The zinnias twirl, in colors so bright,
Tickling the bees with their flirty flight.
A sunflower stands tall, playing peek-a-boo,
While butterflies tease, saying, "Look at you!"

The tomatoes are blushing, oh what a scene,
As cucumbers roll, feeling quite lean.
They laugh at each other, a comical plight,
In this colorful chaos, all feels just right!

The Illumination of Nature's Canvas

In the palette of greens, where laughter does sprout,
The thyme tells stories, and the mint pouts out.
Chives crack a joke, no one is immune,
While onions cry laughter, quite over the moon!

The daisies perform, in their frilly attire,
As bees buzz along, like a comedy choir.
With each silly swish, and each silly sway,
Nature's a stage, in a hilarious play!

Fresh Greens Bathed in Celestial Glow

Beneath gentle rays, the herbs twinkle bright,
The basil gives winks, oh what a sight!
Thyme giggles softly, with a tickle of glee,
While rosemary nods, saying, "Let it be!"

Cilantro spills secrets, oregano grins,
They all take a moment, each sharing their wins.
In this vibrant patch, laughter takes root,
As the garden rejoices, in jest so cute!

Nurtured by Morning's Kiss

In the garden where giggles bloom,
Tiny greens stretch to escape the gloom.
They dance with dew on a playful breeze,
Whispering secrets to the buzzing bees.

The carrots wear hats, oh so neat,
While lettuce laughs, feeling the heat.
Beans tumble down, their strings all a mess,
Making salad day feel like a dress!

Life Unfurls with Each Beat

In the rhythm of growth, a waltz unfolds,
While petals gossip in bright golds.
Pretzel-shaped cucumbers twist with glee,
Chasing after the sun like a wild bee.

The radishes play peekaboo, quite bold,
While spinaches strike poses, feeling gold.
A chorus of greens sings out loud and clear,
As veggies unite for a fun-filled cheer!

Illuminated by Nature's Gaze

The sunflower grins with a toothy grin,
While tiny seeds spin a quirky win.
They juggle with rays from dawn till dusk,
Fashion shows for frogs, what a lively musk!

With dandelions in clownish hats,
And parsley doing pirouettes like sprats.
The whole garden giggles, gives a big cheer,
For every sprout knows they're truly dear!

Beneath the Warmth of Day

Beneath the glow where the giggles play,
Buds are racing to greet the day.
Each leaf is a cartoon, full of zest,
Throwing confetti, they're truly blessed.

Tomatoes bounce with a juicy plot,
Waving hello to the friendly dot.
A dance-off begins with the bumble bee,
In this silly world, they feel so free!

Heralds of Spring in a Bright Horizon

Dandelions dance, it's quite a sight,
Waving to bees, oh what a delight!
Pastel blooms popping, like confetti in air,
Squirrels on branches, without a care.

Grass tickles toes, a soft, green bed,
While ants march around, plans in their head.
A fuzzy caterpillar wearing a grin,
Dreams of becoming a butterfly thin.

Clouds float like marshmallows, fluffy and sweet,
As worms throw a party, the soil's new treat!
The aroma of earth whirls in a tease,
While giggling flowers sway in the breeze.

With sun's playful warmth painting the place,
The garden's a circus, a charming space!
Nature bursts forth in whimsical whirl,
In this joyous jest, let the fun unfurl!

Embers of Warmth Kissing the Earth

Beetles wear shades, strutting so grand,
While spiders spin tales, their webs well planned.
The brook's humming tune plays a cheerful song,
While frogs croak along, thinking they belong.

Clouds drift like rubber ducks on a spree,
As flowers start giggling, 'Oh, look at me!'
A bunny hops past, fed up with the cold,
In search of some warmth, so brave and so bold.

Ladybugs sport polka dots bright,
Chasing down shadows, keeping in sight.
The grasshoppers dance, jump high with glee,
While wishing a sweet pie was found near the tree.

With each joyful laugh shared under the rays,
Every critter and flower joins in for the play!
Nature's a jester, so fun and absurd,
In this riot of life, all joy is stirred!

The Glorious Rise of Tender Greens

Tiny sprouts stretch, a sight to behold,
Like kids on the playground, so eager and bold.
Radishes giggle, their tops poking out,
While carrots underground dance all about.

Petunias are painted, colors so bright,
Playing hide-and-seek with the butterflies' flight.
Lettuce peeks out, with a crisp little laugh,
Wondering aloud who's the silliest half.

In the garden's theater, the sun warming all,
Earthworms gather 'round for the next grand call.
With seedlings all cheering, so spry and so small,
They often forget they're not humans at all!

With joy overflowing, each leaf starts to sway,
In this merry party, no dullness to stay.
The laughter of nature, a playful refrain,
Where every small green knows it has much to gain!

Flourishing Whispers Beneath the Bright

In the garden, whispers of green arise,
As carrots play tag, oh what a surprise!
Peas gossip along, swinging in cheer,
With tulips providing the lovely frontier.

A ladybug's hat is a sight to behold,
While bumblebees buzz with secrets untold.
The clouds giggle softly, a cover for fun,
As seedlings beneath rejoice in the sun.

Pansies parade, with bows in their hair,
While frost-bitten fellows breathe in the air.
Their dreams now igniting, oh how they bloom,
In nature's grand carnival, there's joy to consume!

So raise up your voices, chant low and loud,
For life's a celebration, let's gather a crowd!
With each leaf and petal, a tale we can weave,
In this frolicsome garden, let's always believe!

Juvenile Dreams of Flora

Tiny seeds with grand designs,
They wiggle in their cozy lines.
With whispers from the bright blue sky,
They giggle when the clouds pass by.

Earthworms dance a silly jig,
Thinking they're the dance hall's big.
Roots below in tangled cheer,
Tickling toes of those up here.

A ladybug in polka dots,
Winks at all the pretty pots.
Flowers giggle—oh, what a show,
Twisting in the breeze's flow.

As bees parade with buzzing tunes,
They're feeling bold like big balloons.
In nature's play, we join the fun,
Where every day is just a pun!

Awakening Through Warmth

A sleepy sprout wakes with a yawn,
Sprinkling dreams upon the lawn.
Stretching long beneath the beams,
It giggles, sharing leafy memes.

Frogs jump in with boisterous croaks,
Dressed in suits of leafy cloaks.
The sun asks how to take a seat,
But clouds don't budge—they're much too sweet.

Onward grows the silly green,
Wobbling like a rubber bean.
A flash of color hits the air,
As colors chase without a care!

Gnomes in hats start playing chess,
Making moves that cause a mess.
In laughter, every leaf unfolds,
As nature's humor never molds!

Chasing the Horizon's Glow

A tiny bud on tiptoes stands,
Dreaming big of foreign lands.
It leans and leans to catch a glance,
Of bumblebees that love to dance.

Clouds above are cotton candy,
While raindrops play a game so dandy.
Jubilant roots start doing jumps,
While clovers laugh at all the mumps.

Colors burst like birthday cake,
As petals swirl, it feels like fate.
But then a squirrel on the run,
Trips on grass and ends the fun.

Amid the frolic, streaks of cheer,
Life's a circus—who's the next deer?
Chasing bright rays beneath the sky,
Nature's punchlines fly up high!

In the Embrace of Daybreak

An early bloom peeks from the ground,
In its eyes, the world spins around.
A giddy smile is on display,
As bugs work out their morning play.

With a twitch and a lively shake,
It dances 'round a slice of cake.
Dewdrops giggle, a crystal feast,
While ants parade, not at least.

The grass wears green socks just for fun,
And makes a play to steal the sun.
Each flower sings a silly song,
In harmony, they all belong.

The woodpecker drums a tricky beat,
While daisies sway, with nimble feet.
In morning's glow, they feel alive,
With every giggle, they will thrive!

A Bright Invitation to Blossom

Tiny greens in rows so neat,
Dance along to a rhythm sweet.
With a giggle and a twist,
They shyly beckon, none resist!

A naughty bug comes sneaking by,
In a top hat, oh my, oh my!
He tips his hat, gives a wink,
The greens all blush, but don't overthink!

Unveiling Life Where Light Falls

Little leaves with jaws agape,
Grew a party, no escape!
One's in sequins, one in plaid,
It's the best time they've ever had!

With every ray, they spin and swirl,
A feathery friend gives a twirl.
They giggle so, it's quite a sight,
Feasting on hopes, a pure delight!

The Harmonious Rise of Gentle Greens

Plants unite for a grand ballet,
Wiggling roots in a wild display.
Chasing shadows, they play tag,
But watch out for the playful hag!

She juggles seeds like shiny pearls,
While the greens set off in joyful whirls.
They're singing songs of lazy days,
In a wacky, leafy, sunlight haze!

Daylight's Gentle Touch on the Earth

Sprouts arise with a funky beat,
Tiptoeing soft with nimble feet.
A rhubarb trip, a celery jam,
They rise and shout, "Look at us, fam!"

The sun's a jester, gold and bright,
Flinging light as day turns night.
It's a show where all can join,
A bash where every sprout's the coin!

Buds Beneath a Celestial Glow

In the morning, leaves giggle,
A cucumber whispers, 'I'm a pickle!'
Petals prance with a twist and a twirl,
While broccoli dreams of being a pearl.

Beneath the sky's bright, joking face,
Carrots compete in a silly race.
Spinach sings with a voice so sweet,
Chasing the bees on tiny feet.

Sparkling Dew and Verdant Dreams

Bees in hats buzz with flair,
Grass blades laugh without a care.
Each droplet wears a tiny crown,
As daisies strut around the town.

Tomatoes burst in laughter fits,
While radishes plan their comedy skits.
With playful greens in a jolly sprout,
They dance about, no hint of doubt.

When the Earth Meets the Sky

Clouds tickle the fields with a brush,
As tulips giggle in a friendly hush.
The soil tells jokes, oh what a hoot,
While worms wear ties and laugh in a suit.

Cabbages roll in fits of delight,
Under the stars, they dance at night.
Pumpkins chuckle, they've got it made,
In a patch where all worries fade.

Hope Breathing in Color

Flowers wear socks in a rainbow parade,
Gigantic zucchini, gleefully displayed.
With each bright hue, the plants engage,
A riot of color, a green stage.

Lettuce issues a playful shout,
Play hops through the garden, roundabout.
In this patch of dreams, laughter bursts,
While friendly veggies quench their thirsts.

Lyrical Growth in the Brightness

The garden's jam-packed with a dance,
Wiggly worms take a chance,
With giggles, they twist and glide,
All while the ants scurry wide.

The daisies wear their sunglasses tight,
Chasing shadows that dart in flight,
Gnomes joyfully break out in cheer,
To toast the blooms that disappear.

Bees buzzing like tiny drums,
Fueling laughter with their hums,
They prance around on flowery beds,
While frogs debate on leafy reds.

With every ray, the greens rave on,
As petals sway until they yawn,
In this fiesta, all's awash,
Creating mischief between the squash.

The Awakening of Earthly Splendor

A caterpillar sips his tea,
Wonders what a butterfly will be,
He dreams of wings in pastel shades,
While plotting tricks in leafy glades.

A squirrel's got the latest news,
He's fashioned shoes from morning dew,
With acorns flipping like pancakes wide,
He serves brunch with a cheeky pride.

A daffodil snickers at the rose,
Whispers gossip 'bout her pose,
"I'm the star of this delight,
And you? A bit too sweet for night!"

As dewdrops start their playful fall,
The earth burps loudly, after all,
In this playful, vibrant show,
Every sprout gets to shine and glow.

Petals Unfolding in Golden Hues

The tulips parade in a vibrant line,
Dressed up just to sip sweet wine,
A lily shimmies, flaunts her flair,
While frogs croak tunes, lounging with a stare.

A bumblebee winks, can't help but boast,
"I'll serve you brunch, let's have a toast!"
With daisies cheerleading all around,
Their pom-poms sway with joy profound.

Cabbages squeeze in a goofy dance,
Swapping partners without a chance,
While carrots root for the spinning peas,
In this wacky tale that brings us glee.

As colors blend in a playful whirl,
Each petal giggles, gives a twirl,
In this folly of nature's spree,
Nothing's serious, all's just glee!

A Symphony of Light Beneath Leaves

The trees conspire to tickle the breeze,
Rustling secrets of giggling bees,
A sunflower sways, cracking a grin,
"Who needs crowns when I can win?"

Mushrooms popping with hats on high,
Tell tales to each passing fly,
While the grass plays hopscotch with dew,
A raucous party, just us two!

The clouds drop in, for a laugh or two,
Spilling sprinkles of rainbow hue,
A plucky crow joins the upbeat chat,
"Caw! Caw! I heard that joke, how about that?"

As all the colors jump and sing,
It's a jubilee fit for a king,
In this realm where giggles thrive,
Nature dances, oh, how they jive!

Growing Joy in the Day's Embrace

Little green heads popping up high,
Reaching for giggles, oh my oh my!
They wave to the clouds in playful delight,
Dancing around, what a silly sight!

Worms in their coats do a wiggly jig,
While ants in a line plan a grand gig.
Nature's parade is a delightful mess,
With sunshine dripping and no time to rest!

It's a party of buds, growing wild with cheer,
Twirling and whirling as friends far and near.
The sunbeams tickle with a fizzy flair,
While laughter erupts from the breezy air!

No worries of weeds, just a frolicsome scene,
Patches of joy in a vibrant routine.
With each little sprout, a new joke awaits,
As the earth bursts into merriment fates!

Knots of Life Unfurling Gently

In the damp earth, giggles grow tight,
Twisting and turning, it's a bit of a sight.
With every tangle, a chuckle appears,
As life takes to knots, shedding old fears!

Chubby little roots in their dance,
Twirling about, in a comical trance.
Bouncing around with every small twist,
Whispering secrets that we can't resist!

Little green leaves poke their heads more,
Giving a wave like they often adore.
"Hey look at us, we're so very spry!"
While breezes blow kisses as they shyly fly!

It's a rope of cackles, a knot-so-serious game,
Life's budding humor is never the same.
As nature unwinds with a tickle and tease,
Join in the laughter with the rustling leaves!

The Morning's Touch on Budding Hearts

Kissed by the dawn, the blooms do smile,
Stretching and yawning in their quirky style.
With petals awash in a giggly hue,
They sway and bend like they're sharing a clue!

Puddles of joy with reflections that twinkle,
Sprouts share their secrets, a playful sprinkle.
The breeze carries jokes in a gentle hush,
While bees chuckle softly with a buzzing rush!

Poking their heads from soft earthy beds,
Chomping on sunlight with funny little threads.
"Did you hear the one about the budding rose?"
It's all about laughter, as everybody knows!

As morn paints the world in a colorful spree,
Life grows brighter, playful as can be.
With every bright shimmer, joy breaks like dawn,
Each sprout tells a tale with a giggle and yawn!

Bright Horizons on New Growth

Chasing the daylight, the shoots all race,
Wiggling their green hands in a silly embrace.
Each new leaf shouts, "Look, isn't this grand?"
While the flowers throw confetti all over the land!

The soil whispers tales of laughter and fun,
As roots dive deeper, no need to run.
Jokes bloom like daisies in whimsical style,
Encouraging all to hang out for a while!

Chirping with glee, the critters convene,
For the grand unveiling of the liveliest scene.
Every bud is a punchline, bright with a grin,
Laughing together as they begin to spin!

Horizons stretch wide with colors so bold,
Leaves flutter and whisper, sharing stories untold.
In the garden of giggles, each day feels right,
New growth brings laughter, pure-hearted delight!

The Promise in Every Ember

In the garden where giggles play,
Tiny greens peek out to say,
"We're ready! Toss us some sun!"
While worms dance, just for fun.

A beet's wearing a silly hat,
A radish claims it's where it's at,
With roots that wiggle, oh so bright,
They throw a party under night.

Chubby cheeks of peas so round,
In their own band, they make a sound,
With a rhythm, oh-so sweet,
They stomp their feet, oh what a treat!

The carrots, orange and so spry,
Do cartwheels as they wave goodbye,
For when the raccoons drop by,
It's a comedy in the sky.

Unfolding Under Heaven's Watch

Each petal wakes with sleepy yawns,
While bees perform their buzzing brawns,
The daisies laugh in polka dots,
As drizzles fall in tiny pots.

A tomato thinks it's quite the star,
With grand designs, it plans to spar,
But waits too long, and what a twist,
A squirrel steals it from the mist!

The cucumbers play hide and seek,
In a game that's rather cheeky,
Yet when they trip, with one great flop,
The gardener's laughter just won't stop!

A flower jokes about its hue,
It wonders why it's not a shoe,
But blooms with glee, a sight so true,
A garden full of laughs anew.

Golden Rays on New Beginnings

Under giggles of a morning kiss,
Where leaves do shimmy, none will miss,
A little sprout in quite the tizz,
Yells, "Look at me, I'm in showbiz!"

A beetle dons a tiny suit,
Strutting proud with big ol' roots,
Stars in its eyes, it starts to prance,
While bunnies join in the dance!

With every bit of wiggle and shake,
The garden's got its own earthquake,
And as the seeds begin to rise,
They break the ground with clever lies.

The lettuce keeps a gourmet's range,
While shouting, "Come, let's interchange!"
In this wild and wacky sprout fest,
The joy of life is at its best!

Laughter of the Morning Glow

Fresh buds are waking with a grin,
While giggles echo from within,
Carrots twist in a silly line,
Saying, "Look, I'm the best design!"

The raindrops drop like jolly clowns,
Tickling all from twigs to crowns,
And then a bunny hops in place,
As if to join this silly race.

With every shake and cheerful peep,
The garden's secrets start to creep,
A tiny shoot plays hopscotch here,
While ladybugs spread lots of cheer.

So let the mock-lettuce take a bow,
And let the daisies all avow,
That in this patch of joyful flow,
It's laughter leading the great show!

Whispered Hope Beneath the Canopy

In the shade of a tree, a squirrel danced,
While birds chattered gossip, as if entranced.
A slug wore a top hat, slick and quite neat,
Complaining about how slow was his feat.

The flowers giggled in colors so bright,
Tickling the grass in a ticklish flight.
A caterpillar dreamed of being a butterfly,
But tripped with a sigh, oh me, oh my!

The worms threw a party, all muddy and glum,
With beats from the root, and a thumping drum.
They wiggled and jiggled, feeling so spry,
While moles in the back whispered, "Give it a try!"

And so beneath branches, goofy and bold,
Nature's fun antics continue, behold!
For laughter is growing, both silly and spry,
In the heart of the green where the critters lie.

Blooming Under the Radiant Sky

Petals were painted with giggles and cheer,
As daisies wore shades made of sunshine's smear.
A bee in a bowtie buzzed round the blooms,
Announcing a party amidst floral fumes.

The tulips debated, which color looks best,
While lilacs just lazed in their sweet floral nest.
A rose donned a crown, feeling quite grand,
Said, "Petal power rules this blooming land!"

While ants in a line marched like a parade,
Each one with a crumb, their own food brigade.
They danced on the garden path, slowly, quite spry,
Even grumpy old toads felt a twinkle nearby.

So under the azure, all life took a chance,
To sway in the wind, and to shuffle and dance.
In fields of laughter, they found their own sky,
With blooms and with giggles, oh my, oh my!

Awakening Green in Soft Embrace

A rabbit in pajamas hopped by with a cheer,
Sampling dandelions, his favorite veneer.
The grass giggled softly, tickling his feet,
As frogs croaked a tune from their lily pad seat.

A fox in a bow, all dressed up for a ball,
Swayed with a beetle, who laughed really small.
They curled in the daisies, quite dapper and spry,
As clouds above whispered, "Oh my, oh my!"

And out popped a mushroom with spots just so red,
Telling tall tales of the ducks in his bed.
The crocus blushed warmly, feeling quite shy,
As sunbeams winked merrily from up in the sky.

So life all around, in this soft, funny show,
Awakens in laughter, as creatures say, "Go!"
They leap and they twirl, lost in their spree,
In the lush, silly world, just as happy as can be.

Brightness Through Tender Leaves

A butterfly flitted with grace and delight,
Trying to coax a caterpillar to flight.
"Come join the fun!" she called, flapping her wings,
While ants on the ground planned most silly things.

The trees whispered secrets to each little stem,
As they chuckled at two bees, a loyal old gem.
They'd dance in the wind over petals so bright,
Adventurous spirits spread joy in their flight.

Little ladybugs played hide and seek fast,
Counting on flowers to share in their cast.
The wind tossed its hat, swirling leaves in the air,
As laughter erupted from everywhere there.

Under bright canopies, shenanigans bloom,
In colors and giggles, dispelling all gloom.
For each tiny critter knows, yes indeed,
That joy multiplies when you plant a good seed!

Tender Life Beneath the Sphere

In the garden where giggles grow,
Worms dance like they're in a show.
Daisies wear crown-like hats,
While broccoli wears pants in spats.

Tiny ants march in a line,
Debating what's for lunch and dine.
Bees buzz with a comic tone,
While cabbage rolls up, still alone.

The carrots tug their roots with pride,
Claiming they are the veggie guide.
Tomatoes blush in the bright light,
As radishes giggle, taking flight.

Underneath the sun's warm grin,
Garden jokes bloom thick as skin.
Planting fun in rows and rows,
Nature's comedy, how it grows!

In the Glow of Vitality

A flower sneezes, pollen sprays,
While the tulips giggle in the rays.
Dandelions blow wishes like seeds,
With each puff, they plant their deeds.

The mushrooms wear hats just for flair,
While grasshoppers leap high in the air.
The prancing peacock struts with pride,
But slips on a snail—what a wild ride!

Chickens join in a laugh-out-loud,
Telling tales to impress the crowd.
With every hop and skip they make,
The garden's humor's hard to shake.

In this haven of quirk and fun,
Every vine shimmies in the sun.
Planting smiles on every face,
In this wild and wacky place!

Awareness in Every Green Fold

The leaves whisper secrets to the breeze,
Talking gossip about the bees.
Grass claims it's the softest seat,
While flowers declare they can't be beat.

A little sprite dances on a stem,
Telling stories, loud and grand.
Cucumbers claim they're quite the catch,
But zucchinis think they're the best match.

The soil chuckles, rich and deep,
While seeds plot mischief while they sleep.
Every sprout's a jokester, bold,
As tales of green and laughter unfold.

With humor sprouting 'neath the sky,
Nature's punchlines never die.
A quirky, lively green abode,
Where every root has jokes bestowed!

Energized by the Morning Chorus

Morning's chorus sings with glee,
A symphony of rustling leaves, you see.
The daisies dance, their petals sway,
As morning glories shout, "Hooray!"

The sun tickles every little sprout,
As ladybugs scuttle about.
With a hop and a laugh, the clovers cheer,
Making every dew drop crystal clear.

The frogs croak out a goofy song,
While butterflies flutter and dance along.
The garden's rhythm pulses bright,
Creating smiles from dawn 'til night.

Nature's laughter fills the air,
With joyous bursts beyond compare.
Every creature shares the sound,
In this playful world, joy abounds!

Nature's Rebirth After the Chill

In the garden, a sneeze, oh what a sight,
A bump in the ground says, 'Guess who's polite?'
Little green hats, sprouting heads all around,
Climbing up high, dancing, oh how they bound!

The critters awake, all shaky and spry,
Worms in tuxedos, oh my, oh my!
Rabbits in bowties, they hop and they prance,
Celebrating spring with a fumble-filled dance!

Transcendent Touch of Daylight

A bright face appears, the world wakes with a grin,
Tickling the clouds and making them spin.
Plants reach and stretch, with a giggle they sprout,
Whispering secrets, they're ready to shout!

Bees buzzing around, oh what a chirp,
Wearing tiny goggles, they're ready to burp.
Flowers in ties, they're having a ball,
Each petal a joke, but no one will stall!

Renewal in the Warmth of Day

Bouncing little seeds, they roll with great cheer,
Saying to dirt, 'We're glad you're still here!'
With a wink and a wiggle, they push their way high,
Looking for sun, giving clouds the sly eye.

Laughter in leaves as they tickle the sky,
Trees whisper jokes, oh me, oh my!
A choir of crickets, they chirp out of tune,
But who needs a symphony when life's in full bloom?

The Joy of Life in Vibrant Shades

Colors burst forth in a riotous show,
As if a painter sneezed, and the colors did flow.
Dandelions giggle, wearing crowns on their head,
While violets wink, 'We're sweet, not just red!'

Squirrels in shorts, a nutty parade,
Chasing their tails in grass that won't fade.
The world in a whirl, such a funny display,
With nature in high spirits, let's brighten the day!

Nature's Embrace Under Celestial Glow

Tiny tummies twist and turn,
Beneath a hug of warmth they yearn.
Wiggling worms in a mudpie race,
Dance like they've found the perfect place.

Bouncing beetles in a conga line,
Roiling rascals having a good time.
Fuzzy bumbles buzzing around,
Looking for fun in the grass they found.

Silly snails try to speed walk by,
With secret dreams of being spry.
They'll race the breeze and hop with glee,
To win the prize—a leaf for tea!

The world's a giggle, full of cheer,
Join the party; don't just leer!
Nature's laughter fills the air,
With a twist, a skip, and a funny hair.

The Dance of Hope in Every Leaf

Little green hats on a windy street,
Swaying to beats of nature's heartbeat.
A ladybug leads with a bold little jig,
While ants join in, feeling quite big.

Poppy petals take a twirl and spin,
Winking at worms as the fun begins.
Caterpillars dreaming of being quite grand,
In the twisty dance, they hold each hand.

Dewdrops laugh as they bounce and gleam,
Making the flowers laugh in a dream.
Petals fold their arms, say "Look at me!"
While grasshoppers laughingly shout with glee.

What a lively, vibrant cast!
Nature's the stage, and the fun is vast!
Join in the jig, shake off your frown,
As we dance in circles wearing green crowns.

Dappled Gold on New Green

Bouncing beams land with a cheeky grin,
Painting shadows where the fun begins.
Chasing after butterflies in a flash,
While daisies laugh and make a splash.

A peek-a-boo game with the clouds above,
Where the daisies whisper, "We're all in love!"
Silly petals tickled by a breeze,
Doing the twist with the greatest ease.

Branches wobble as squirrels play tag,
On swing-like limbs, they like to brag.
"I'm the fastest!" and "You can't catch me!"
Nature's playground, let your spirit be free!

A concert of chirps, a giggle or two,
Bouncing by, that busy bee crew.
With dappled gold shining down below,
Feeling the fun in the friendly glow.

Tender Veins of Life Unfurling

Sprightly tendrils stretch and tease,
Climbing high at a playful breeze.
Each leaf a quirk, a wink, a nod,
In this wild world, go on, applaud!

Buds are blushing, it's flower power,
Raising their heads in the sunny hour.
Frogs wear crowns, they leap with delight,
"Wanna join our party? It's outta sight!"

Mischievous roots play a game of hide,
While the flowers prance with unbridled pride.
Ticklish petals giggle all day,
With every bounce in a cabaret sway.

Nature's a circus, come take a seat,
Watch the show where laughter's sweet.
In every corner, joy and fun,
In this merry dance, we've only begun.

Nature's Gentle Warmth Unfolds

A gentle touch from up above,
Illuminates the earth like love.
The plants wake up, with silly grins,
Stretching limbs like they just won bins.

The bees are buzzing, oh what a sight,
Wearing tiny goggles, ready for flight.
They dance around with such a flare,
As flowers giggle without a care.

The grass is green, the worms are bold,
They wiggle poppin' like they've been told.
Each blade a carpet, a comfy seat,
For critters planning a party meet.

The clouds above, in fluffy fluff,
Wonder if the day is good enough.
They sip their tea, and watch below,
As nature's antics start the show.

Seeds of Dreams in Warm Embrace

Tiny specks, what do they know?
Hiding deep in warming show.
They whisper secrets, plotting schemes,
To wake and bloom, fulfill their dreams.

With dirt as pillows and roots as beds,
They chatter softly, sharing threads.
"When will we pop? When's our debut?"
The earth just laughs, 'Soon, it's true!'

A sprinkle here, a giggle there,
Water drips in dandelion hair.
"Is this a spa? Came here for fun!"
"Oh, just a little time in the sun!"

So up they stretch, like kids at play,
Embracing the warmth of the day.
With every tick of Mother's clock,
They strive to outgrow the garden rock.

The Dance of Light on Fresh Growth

A spotlight shines on vibrant hues,
Greeners wink like they've got the news.
Chasing shadows, they curtsy low,
"Join the show, it's our time to glow!"

With twirls and sways, the branches tease,
A game with wind, a breeze to please.
The daisies giggle, wearing crowns,
As ants parade in their tiny gowns.

The morning laughs, oh what a scene,
As sprouts compete for the biggest green.
"Who can stretch the highest today?"
The tallest one shouts, "I lead the play!"

But one little shoot, feeling quite bold,
Declared, "I'm the best, or so I'm told!"
And in a flash, it dances light,
Leaving the others in sheer delight.

Eager Shoots in Dawn's Caress

When morning whispers, the fun begins,
Little green hats pop on winds.
They bounce awake with chirps and chirrups,
Like fluffy pillows with little hiccups.

The dew is laughing, giggling on leaves,
Playing hide and seek with the little thieves.
"Oh look, a raindrop, quick, take cover!"
But oh, it's just juice from their brother!

Each sprout is proud, in a neat little row,
Posing stiff, like a nature show.
"Look at us now, all straight and tall!"
But one little guy tripped and took a fall.

"Oops! Not me!" he squeals with zest,
"Just practicing for your garden fest!"
So laughter spreads, in this playful place,
Where every shoot wears a happy face.

Enchanted Growth in Radiant Light

In a patch where greens collide,
A carrot wore a leafy tie.
The radish danced with glee and pride,
While peas formed lines to reach the sky.

A cabbage snorted, full of mirth,
Claiming he knew how to sway.
The beets all laughed, for what it's worth,
The cabbage just made veggie hay.

The herbs held hands, a fragrant crew,
Singing tunes of mint and thyme.
In this patch, friendships grew,
All wrapped in joy, a veggie rhyme.

As flowers twirled in gentle style,
Petals fluttering in the breeze.
The soil chuckled with its smile,
A comedic act, nature's tease.

Life's Vibrance Under Warm Skies

A little seed took quite a leap,
Declared to grow ten inches tall.
But soon it found, it wasn't steep,
Just a mole who liked to crawl!

The daisies wore their brightest hats,
Boasting colors to the max.
While ants held tiny dance-offs,
Creating their own silly tracks.

Bumblebees buzzed off-key tunes,
They swirled like dancers, less like bees.
Their moves could make the daisies swoon,
But sometimes led to big mishaps, you see!

And in the shade, a gnome stood still,
Telling jokes to mushrooms near.
His humor wasn't such a thrill,
But even fungi had to cheer.

Warmth's Magic on Green Dreams

In a garden full of fluff,
A pumpkin tried on shimmery shoes.
His friends all laughed, they'd had enough,
As he twirled, he'd often bruise!

The squash had plans, oh what a fête,
To celebrate with cake and cheer.
A confetti storm, oh, it was great,
Until the cat crashed in, oh dear!

The tomatoes giggled, round and red,
They rolled around, a jolly sight.
The lettuce sighed, "Can't we be fed?"
But instead, they danced into the night.

With each new sprout and tiny bud,
The laughter grew, the fun did swell.
In every root, a story's thud,
Nature's jest, a joyous spell.

The Chorus of Blooming Colors

A host of colors, a raucous crowd,
The flowers shouted, "Look at me!"
Tulips bowing, oh so proud,
While daisies sought more novelty.

The butterflies joined in the game,
Flapping wings like confetti flies.
A poppy blushed, but was quite lame,
For she tripped o'er her own surprise!

The violets chuckled in the shade,
Painting the air with laughing scents.
Each bloom a story, sweet parade,
Under the sky, their giggle tents.

And as the dusk began to sing,
The blooms all tossed their heads in fun.
A choir of colors, oh what a fling,
Their laughter echoed, day was done.

Radiant Beginnings of Life Above

In the garden, all things sprout,
With glee they wiggle, twist about.
A flower yawns, a leaf gives a shout,
'Is it morning? Let's party, no doubt!'

The veggies dance, what a sight,
Carrots doing the tango, oh what delight!
Peas in a pod, snug and tight,
Laughing at squirrels that leap in fright.

A daisy wears a bright sun hat,
Announcing loudly, 'I'm where it's at!'
While a beet blushes, shy and flat,
'Can you believe I'm such a sprat?'

In this patch, joy's on display,
Nature's humor come out to play.
Every sprout and bloom has its say,
Making silly memories every day.

Lush New Life in Dappled Light

Underneath the leafy trees,
Worms are racing, hoping to please.
'Who's the fastest?' one queries with ease,
While ants march on like little CEOs.

Butterflies flutter in bright ballet,
On flowers' backs, they sway and sway.
'A rose is a rose,' one bee did say,
'But I prefer the daisies all day!'

Pumpkins plotting in a vine embrace,
'We'll be the stars of Halloween's race!'
Tomatoes giggle, 'We'll win with grace,
Dressed in red, we'll take first place!'

Nature's humor sings in the breeze,
Every little plant does as it please.
With comical quirks, life's a tease,
In this realm where joy's like summer cheese.

The Celestial Warming of the Earth

When warmth arrives, the world does cheer,
Ants have a party, bring out the beer!
'Who's got snacks?' shouts out a deer,
While flowers bloom, in strokes so clear.

A robin croons, 'Is it time to sing?'
While worms prepare for a wormy fling.
Daffodils laugh, 'Look at us swing!
We're the champions of spring's bling-bling!'

Cucumbers cracked jokes about their shape,
'We're the pickles of life, berry great tape!'
Radishes roll, no need for escape,
'Join the fun, there's no need to gape!'

Every critter joins the fleet,
In this show where humor is neat.
Nature's stage is a merry beat,
With laughter echoing from every seat.

Shimmer of Light on Sprouting Dreams

Tiny seeds in the soil do plot,
'Let's break through, give it all we've got!'
Their dreams of growing—what a hot shot!
Bringing laughter, stir and tot.

A sunflower peeks, his head held high,
'Look at me, I'm the king, oh my!'
While carrots giggle, 'Just pass us by,
We're underground, still aiming for the sky!'

A dainty breeze carries jokes all around,
As ladybugs dance, they leap and bound.
'We won't stop till we're sunrise crowned,'
Whispering secrets in spins profound.

As every leaf rustles with glee,
This scene's a comic jubilee.
Nature's laughter is wild and free,
Sprouting tales for all to see.

In the Warmth of a New Dawn

In the morning glow, giggles rise,
Little green hats wear quirky ties.
Wiggling roots do tango in the dirt,
While ladybugs cheer in vibrant skirts.

A tiny sprout with dreams so grand,
Says, "I'll grow taller than the stand!"
With worms offering dance tips, quite absurd,
They whirl and twirl, oh, how they blurred!

Blades of grass play peek-a-boo,
Tickling feet in funny shoes.
While daisies chuckle, bright and bold,
They gossip sweetly, stories told.

With each new day, they jest and tease,
"Why do birds sound like a sneeze?"
In the party of growth, laughter is shared,
Underneath blooms, no one is scared.

Nature's Palette in Vibrant Confetti

Crayons dropped from the sky of blue,
Painting flowers in every hue.
Butterflies flutter with giddy spins,
Suggesting plants wear silly grins.

A daffodil in a striped bow tie,
Proclaims, "I'm here to catch your eye!"
While bees buzz tunes of a humorous beat,
Trying their best not to move their feet.

The wind whispers jokes through the trees,
Leaves giggle and sway in the breeze.
An acorn quips, "I'm not just a snack,"
"Someday I'll be a mighty oak, never lack!"

In this garden of mirth and delight,
Nature holds its own comedy night.
Each sprout and bloom a punchline, see?
They thrive on laughter, wild and free.

Joyful Growth Beneath the Awakening Light

Poking through soil with mischief in mind,
Tiny greens giggle, "We're one of a kind!"
A radish, blushing, squeaks quite shy,
While petals of zinnias dance up high.

"Is that a worm, or a wriggly dash?"
"Let's race him home, oh, in a flash!"
With a wobbling beet in a friendly grin,
They root for fun, they can't help but win!

A chorus of crickets joins the fray,
Singing of sunshine, hip-hip-hooray!
The clouds roll in, a blurry face,
Shouting, "Surprise!" in a fluffy embrace.

And when rain drops fall like silly whacks,
They splash and giggle, no holding backs.
Each drop a joke on sprightly ground,
In this playful patch, joy is abound!

The Radiant Symphony of New Life

A frog in a pot sings, "Hippity hop!"
As blooms break out, there's no sign to stop.
Grasshoppers strum on blades so fine,
While ladybugs dance like they're on cloud nine.

With buds that chuckle, "Let's start a band!"
Bees play the drums with their buzzing hand.
Each flower takes center stage to pose,
As laughter cascades, how joyfully it grows!

Petunias sway to a floral tune,
While daisies prance under a cotton-candy moon.
The breeze blows softly, tickling the leaves,
In this garden where mirth never leaves.

Rabbits tap dance in a playful race,
Each hop a giggle, a wild embrace.
In nature's orchestra, each note a delight,
Their ensemble thrives in pure, happy light.

A Tapestry of Light and Life

A cold little seed, I waited down low,
With dreams of a dance, would I ever grow?
Then came a tickle, from up above,
I giggled and stretched, what a myth of love!

The sky said, "Get up, you funny little sprout,"
"There's a world of jazz waiting to shout!"
So I spun and I twirled, in my leafy attire,
Hoping to impress, but tripped on my wire!

Oh, the worms rolled their eyes, they'd seen it all,
As I flopped in the dirt, doing my fall!
Yet laughter resounded through the garden fair,
A chorus of blooms joined in the air!

With every bloom booming, and colors so bright,
I learned that my antics chase away the night!
So here's to the little ones, dancing with glee,
In this tapestry, we laugh and we be!

The Gentle Kiss of Daylight

A dandelion blew with a puff and a cheer,
"Wake up, sleepy heads, it's time to appear!"
But petals were groggy, night's blanket was snug,
So they rolled in their quilts, in a botanical hug!

"Oh hurry!" cried Clover, "Don't be such a slug!"
With a grin and a wiggle, she gave them a tug.
"Let's stretch and laugh; the new day's a gift,
Or else we'll miss out on the sun's funny lift!"

With giggles and grumbles, the garden awoke,
A parade of green waves, no one left broke.
From daisies to roses, they joined in a line,
Wobbling and wiggling, so silly and fine!

And when the bright beams tickled each face,
They danced in delight, a garden embrace!
For life's just a romp when laughter's the way,
In this silly tableau, we welcome the day!

Unfurling Dreams in the Warmth

A sprout had a secret, it whispered in shades,
Dreams of a party where sunlight cascades.
It rolled with the breezes, it danced left and right,
"I'll twirl with the bugs; oh, what a delight!"

But there came a wise snail with spectacles too,
"Dear sprout," he said, "You must know this is true:
Fungi have parties that truly take flight,
So polished those gills and prepare for a night!"

So the sprouts took a vote, and they polled the whole patch,
With roses as DJs, and lilies to hatch!
"Let's groove 'til we droop," they all chattered with glee,
While earthworms wormed their way through the spree!

Thus the daisies counted; they counted till noon,
With petals adorned like a fluffy balloon.
When evening rolled in with a glittery sigh,
The garden ignited with laughter that spry!

Hope Sprouts in the Heart of Day

In a kingdom of green, where giggles abound,
A thought popped like popcorn, exclaiming its sound!
"I'm more than a leaf; I'm a comedian, see?
With roots that tickle and a stem full of glee!"

All flowers gathered, some white and some blue,
Said, "Tell us a joke; we could use a good brew!"
So the little green marvel cleared its tiny throat,
"I'm a garden of laughs, come join in my note!"

The bees filled with buzz, they couldn't believe,
Laughter was blooming; it made them all leave!
And with every good chuckle, through sunlight they soared,
In this zany little patch, joy was restored!

Now each day unfolds with a whimsical crew,
Who sprout with ambition, as flowers all do!
In the heart of this garden, giggles ignite,
Where laughter and hope bathe the day in pure light!

www.ingramcontent.com/pod-product-compliance
Lightning Source LLC
Chambersburg PA
CBHW070325120526
44590CB00017B/2820